The Titanic Story

The Titanic Story

David Hutchings

The
History
Press

Also in this series:

◄◄
RMS Titanic, *Cherbourg*.
('Au Revoir to the Old
World' by Ken Marschall)

◄
Foredeck of RMS Titanic.
(Ulster Folk & Transport
Museum)

►
RMS Olympic *returns
to Belfast after losing a
propeller blade. Work
continues on RMS* Titanic
(right). (Harland and Wolff)

First published in the United Kingdom in 2008 by
The History Press
The Mill · Brimscombe Port · Stroud
Gloucestershire · GL5 2QG

Reprinted 2010, 2012, 2017

British Library Cataloguing in Publication Data
A catalogue record for this book is available from the
British Library.

ISBN 978-0-7509-4845-6

For Josh and Reece

Typeset in Syntax.
Typesetting and origination by
The History Press.
Printed and bound in China.

CONTENTS

Throughout history there have been many famous ships that have crossed the oceans of the world: some famous for their speed; some for their size; some for their luxury; and some for their fate.

It was fate which decreed that one great liner would achieve notoriety, infamy almost, that would increase as the years passed by. The effects that directly resulted from this ship's passing are still with us – a lasting legacy of a lesson harshly learnt through the experience, loss and despair of others.

In today's world, often ignorant of shipping, this particular vessel has been often erroneously described as 'a cruise ship'; 'the largest, most luxurious liner *ever* built' and 'out for the record'.

She was certainly not a 'cruise ship' (cruising had many years to go before it became popular for the masses). She was an ocean-going liner, designed to provide a regular service across the North Atlantic as a bridge between two great English-speaking countries. Although she was the largest vessel at the time of her appearance, she would, within a few

➤
RMS Titanic, *a few days before her launch.* (Ulster Folk & Transport Museum)

months, have conceded this accolade to imminent German ships. She was not designed to be fast, but designed for a comfort that could only be bought at a speed lesser than that of the hectic record-breakers of the time.

She was indeed luxurious: rich panels (some inlaid with mother-of-pearl), thick carpets, an à la carte restaurant, an elegant Palm Court complete with after-dinner music, a gymnasium, swimming pool and Turkish bath – and a reputation for being 'unsinkable'. The manner of this ship's passing and the enormous effect she has had on our safety at sea today means she has deservedly become a great British icon.

That ship was *Titanic*.

ACKNOWLEDGEMENTS

➤
Titanic *survivor Edith Haisman (ncé Brown) in later years. She died on 20 January 1997 aged 100.* (Photograph by the author)

The author would like to thank Valerie Barnish, Mark Chirnside, the late Bertram Dean, the late Millvina Dean, Jack Eaton, Charles Haas, David Haisman, the late Edith Haisman, the late Eva Hart, Dorothy Kendal, Betty MacQuitty, the late William MacQuitty, Henry Pugh, Mark Slade, Brian Ticehurst and Ron Williams.

The author has aimed to acknowledge all sources of the illustrations that he has used.

If any of these pictures are improperly credited then I sincerely apologise and hope to make amends in future editions.

'I'll see you in New York!'
Thomas Brown's parting words to his daughter, Edith, who survived the sinking of *Titanic*.

◄
Six-year-old William MacQuitty, who attended the launch of Titanic *with his father, James.* (By kind permission of the Estate of William MacQuitty)

◄◄
Titanic *in dock at Belfast.* (Author's collection)

ix

Hundreds upon hundreds of ocean liners have plied the maritime highways of the world and it has fallen to a few of these to achieve a lasting fame. This small book is about one of the most famous of these ships ever to have sailed the seas and is aimed at those wishing to know a little of the basics as to why this particular vessel, the Royal Mail Steamship *Titanic*, was built and what gave her a place in history.

There have been larger liners since and, in today's world, larger cruise ships, and there have been shipwrecks that caused greater losses of life (*General von Steuben*, *Wilhelm Gustloff*, *Doña Paz*, to name but three), so why is *Titanic* so special?

At the time of her loss, on 15 April 1912, not only was she the largest liner in the world, but she was new and she was on her maiden voyage. *Titanic* was special because she was the very visible epitome of British engineering, an engineering that had dominated the world for decades, producing 50 per cent of the world's ships, railways and bridges. Great Britain's Royal Navy was, through a deliberate policy, as big as the next two largest navies combined and the appearance of any new engineering feat that would be a world-beater (an attribute that had come to be expected from Britain's industrial might) in speed or size was therefore eagerly awaited by the world-wide citizens of 'The Empire on which the sun never set'.

The disaster that overtook the *Titanic* represented not only a great loss of human life but also the loss of an empire's prestige and self-confidence. The new legislation that resulted from her loss was far-reaching and improvements on that initial legislation

➤➤
RMS Olympic, *one of White Star Line's Olympic-class liners, portrayed in a rough sea.* (Artist unknown, author's collection)

R.M.S. OLYMPIC IN MID-OCEAN

are still being made today. *Titanic* was a sharp lesson in human behaviour and the self-assured arrogance of wealth that gave this era its label of The Gilded Age. Never again would mankind be so sure of its achievements and the materially based security that came as a result. The First World War that erupted two years after the liner's loss would finally ram this lesson home in a brutal and bloody way.

Ever since Norse adventurers discovered the North American continent, Europeans have held it as an ambition to conquer and colonise that enormous stretch of land and exploit its vast natural resources.

Over the centuries the need to transport settlers across the 3,000 miles of challenging and often violent waters of the North Atlantic – the Western Ocean – and to return with precious minerals and furs caused the design of ships gradually to evolve.

The Industrial Revolution saw iron replacing wood as steam-driven machinery found purpose in factories and mines. In this revolution coal was king and was needed in great quantities to generate the all-powerful steam in ever-increasing pressures to drive machinery. Labour was

Skilled draughtsmen at Harland and Wolff in Belfast, working on long drawing benches, detail the structure, machinery and electrical layouts of the new vessels.
(Ulster Folk & Transport Museum)

thus mechanised and output and profits increased. Railways spread their influence over the land, and at sea, during the fourth decade of the nineteenth century, ships became independent of the wind as improving steam engines replaced canvas, enabling vessels to sail on predetermined courses and keep to timetables.

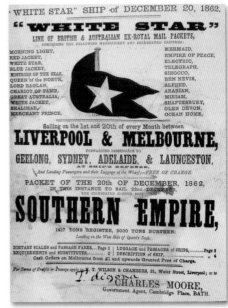

To *Sirius*, a steam-driven paddle steamer, fell the honour of being the first steamship to cross the Atlantic without the aid of a sail, taking eighteen-and-a-half days to complete the journey. Following her into New York by a mere few hours paddled the *Great Western*, the first great ship to be conceived by the brilliant Victorian engineer Isambard Kingdom Brunel – a ship specifically designed for the North Atlantic route. Having been delayed by a fire that nearly claimed her designer's life, the ship had taken fifteen days, sailing two days after the *Sirius*, thus setting a criteria for fast crossings and records.

While the *Sirius* had run seriously short of coal by the time of her arrival, Brunel's *Great Western* still had 200 tons in her bunkers, thereby proving that steamships *could* carry enough fuel for the crossing without resorting to sail. This led the way to passages being able to run on a regular timetable.

The White Star Line was founded by Thomas Henry Ismay in 1869. (Author's collection)

White Star's house-flag was bought from a sailing ship company. (Author's collection)

Brunel's next ship was the iron-built, propeller-driven *Great Britain,* the first true ocean liner. His two fine but mismatched vessels were unable to win the crucial mail contract and it fell to Nova Scotian Samuel Cunard and three British partners to propose a line of four-paddle steamers that could provide the regular service that a postal contract demanded.

Cunard's line, the British and North American Royal Mail Steam Packet Company, built on its success. Competitors fell by the wayside, but one other line matched and lasted the course: the Oceanic Steamship Navigation Company. Popularly known as the White Star Line, the OSNC soon became a serious contender on the North Atlantic route.

The majority of the White Star Line's vessels were built by shipbuilders Harland and Wolff of Belfast. Cabins were larger and more luxurious than their rivals' (with running water and portholes); cabin-class (first-class) accommodation was relocated from aft to amidships; and full-width dining saloons were introduced. However, a larger length-to-breadth ratio earned them the epithet of 'coffin ships'.

▼
The White Star Wharf at Queenstown, 1912, showing the spire-less St Coleman's Cathedral still under construction. (Author's collection)

The line's first ship, the *Oceanic*, appeared in 1871, soon to be followed by the *Baltic*, *Atlantic* and *Pacific*, all of 3,707 gross tons (gt); then *Arctic* and *Adriatic* (3,888gt). They were employed on the company's service from Liverpool to New York via Queenstown (Cobh) in the south of Ireland, then still under British rule.

Rival Collins Line had lost its identically named *Pacific* (without trace in 1856) and *Arctic* (in a collision), so each White Star captain was presented with a letter that exhorted him to use 'due diligence in making a favourable passage' and to 'dismiss from

'. . . concentrat[e] your whole attention upon a cautious, prudent, and ever watchful system of navigation . . . rather than run the slightest risk.'
White Star instructions to its captains in order to try and avoid disasters at sea. (1871)

your mind . . . competitive passages with other vessels'.

Between 1871 and 1875 four of White Star's vessels achieved the speed record, gaining the coveted Blue Ribband of the North Atlantic: *Baltic* (to have originally been named *Pacific* but changed after the loss of the Collins liner of the same name) in 1871, *Adriatic* in 1872, *Britannic* in 1874, followed by *Germanic* in 1875. The latter two were awarded regardless of the tragedy in 1873 when White Star suffered a major disaster: *Atlantic* was wrecked en route to New York in fierce gales and 585 people lost their lives.

A lull then occurred in White Star's contending for the record while the battle was fought out between the Inman, Guion, National and Cunard lines.

White Star's final Ribband competitors were two fine vessels, the *Teutonic* and

Majestic (*c.* 9,680gt) of 1889. Built for easy conversion into Armed Merchant Cruisers (AMCs) by the attachment of cannon on to pads concealed beneath their upper decks, these ships influenced competitive German naval thinking at the highest level.

Teutonic was put on display at the 1889 Naval Review in the Solent. An impressed Kaiser Wilhelm II, the young, new emperor of a recently united Germany, toured the liner, escorted by a proud Thomas Ismay.

Arguably, this friendly visit culminated in a great naval race and, ultimately, fifteen years later contributed to the outbreak of the First World War in 1914.

As demand for Atlantic passages grew, so did the size of ships and the associated development of larger engines. The quest for speed created unwelcome vibration so White Star decided to opt out of the race.

▲
En route to New York in 1873, and with only 127 tons of coal left, the Atlantic *changed course for Halifax, NS, only to be wrecked on Meagher's Rock, Maris Head, with the loss of 585 lives.* (Author's collection)

The company still commissioned fast ships which met the stipulations of Government Mail Contracts, demanding regularity in return for generous subsidies. Their new ships would be fuller in the hull with a subsequent increased carrying capacity, whether cargo or passengers. Travelling at slower speeds than their rivals, this would

▲
Oceanic: *the 'crowning glory of the nineteenth century', as Kaiser Wilhelm II described her at her launch in early 1899.* (Author's collection)

not deter passengers, who instead would be able to indulge in the greater luxury and comfort of passage upon which the line would pride itself.

The first of these comfortable ships was the *Oceanic (II)* of 1899. The liner, although still built as an AMC, sported a lavish interior that included gold-plated light fittings. Her maiden voyage that same August preceded Thomas Ismay's death by three months. His son, J. Bruce, took over the helm. After Ismay Senior's death, *Oceanic*'s planned sistership was cancelled. Had she materialised she would have been named *Olympic*, a name that would remain dormant for another six years.

Three years after his father's death, J. Bruce Ismay reluctantly agreed to enter into negotiations with an extremely wealthy American financier, J. Pierpont Morgan, who had created huge empires based on the combination of steel and railway interests.

Turning his attention to the North Atlantic, Morgan saw that too many ships were plying the route. Resultant tariff wars were crippling the trade and he considered that American goods should be carried in American-controlled ships, not in foreign bottoms.

The 'new vogue among rich Americans for making luxurious transatlantic crossings' spurred him to form an American 'community of interest' encouraging cooperation among competitors. A huge Anglo-American fleet of 120 ships would result by combining the American-flagged American Line (ex-Inman Line) with the British Atlantic Transport, Dominion, Leyland and Red Star lines to form the International Mercantile Marine – the IMM.

But the jewels of the British shipping crown still eluded him – the Cunard and White Star Lines.

By 1902 the White Star Line owned four large ships – Celtic, Cedric, Baltic and Adriatic – either in service or pending. (Author's collection)

WHITE STAR LINE
TWIN-SCREW R.M.S. "ADRIATIC."

In 1901 Harland and Wolff's chairman, Lord Pirrie, entered a shipbuilding agreement with the IMM to ensure the future of his shipyard. On Morgan's behalf, Pirrie (a White Star shareholder) approached Ismay and in 1902 White Star was eventually absorbed into the IMM.

A public outcry erupted in Britain; not only was the country losing its most prestigious shipping company, but also a potential maritime force in the event of future conflict. The British government received assurances that White Star ships would still sail under the Red Ensign, be manned by British officers and crew and be made available as AMCs to the British Admiralty if required. Seriously shaken, the government then entered negotiations with the Cunard Line, hoping to dissuade it from joining the combine.

As a result, the government concurred with Cunard that two express liners should be built under favourable loans, receive generous annual subsidies for carrying the Royal Mail and, if the need arose, find well-compensated employment as very fast AMCs. Driven by turbines, they would be the fastest ships in the world yet still be comfortable and, at around 32,000gt and 790ft in overall length, would be the largest, assuaging the most bullish of patriotic jingoists.

These two liners would be the *Lusitania* and *Mauretania* and would successfully wipe the board of any competition for the Blue Ribband.

The Royal Navy had not been slow in adopting the turbine, commissioning the first of a super-class of battleship, HMS *Dreadnought*, which not only gave her

name to the subsequent series of super ships, but also alarmed Germany by the publicised speed of her construction: a year and a day. (Building had actually taken longer but the propaganda was good for the British.)

With the backing of 'serious' American money, Bruce Ismay (now President of the IMM as well as Chairman of White Star Line) was able to plan the future with some considerable confidence. If White Star could not have the fastest ships in the world then they could certainly have the biggest and most luxurious. To this end, in 1906 Ismay famously met with Lord Pirrie at the latter's London mansion, Downshire House, in London's Belgrave Square while the Cunard sisterships were still building.

After-dinner talk centred on ideas from which Lord Pirrie, an experienced naval architect, prepared preliminary sketches of a ship with three funnels; a novel arrangement of two four-cylindered reciprocating engines that exhausted into a low-pressure turbine. It had three propellers, was 880ft long, and had a

▼
With turbines and a revolutionary weaponry arrangement, HMS Dreadnought *rendered all other battleships afloat obsolete overnight.* (Author's collection)

breadth of over 90ft. With gross tonnages of 45,000 the new class would be a world-beater. Luxury would be built in with no expense spared.

Masts were excluded initially, but were reinstated when Bruce Ismay saw the *Mauretania* in New York and was sufficiently impressed.

The first of the proposed Olympic-class ships was to be called *Olympic*, thus resurrecting the name of the abandoned sistership of *Oceanic*. The second ship was named *Titanic*. Later, speculation anticipated a third sister, with rumours of her being named *Gigantic*, in continuance with the Olympian theme.

In 1907 the new Cunarders, *Mauretania* and *Lusitania*, swept the board in a glittering display of size, speed, luxury and bravura – and an unheard-of comfort provided by smooth-running turbine engines. Their high-performance debut would be difficult to follow but the brilliant double act of Pirrie and Ismay was a determined one and had the British public anticipating the Olympic-class arrival with a fervour almost equalling that which fanfared the Cunarders.

White Star could only hope to compete on two of Cunard's levels: size and comfort; luxury would be in excess. Record-breaking would not even enter the equation, unless one ship were set against its own sister (as with the Cunarders, where the enormous expense involved was more than compensated for by the publicity generated, as an eager public followed the construction of the Scottish- and English-built ships).

Other than the commercial gains generated by such competition, this very public demonstration had an added

The Olympic-class's original designer, the Honourable Alexander Carlisle. (Southampton City Museums)

▲
The Arrol gantry had lifts, overhead and side cranes, and sloping walkways that enabled men and materials to access the upper levels of growing ships. (Ulster Folk & Transport Museum)

With the White Star/IMM deal there were neither political nor nationalistic axes to grind. The Americans favoured peace, isolation and luxury, and the new liners would suit these transatlantic inclinations admirably.

Using Pirrie's sketches, the designers of Harland and Wolff calculated, developed, modified and refined ideas until, as a result of their studious deliberations, a general arrangement for the new ships evolved. These were further developed to great detail by the Drawing Offices.

The plans were then replicated by the Mould Loft in chalked, full-size lines on the Loft's wooden floor, where curves were faired and permanently 'scrieved' (scratched) onto the floor, from which wooden templates (moulds) were formed so that steel plates and bars could be shaped, bent and drilled.

political advantage: it demonstrated to the rising ambitions of the German empire that it might be advisable not to 'mix it' with the British, whose empire was eager to show, in peaceful terms, that Britain still built the best – and that the best could be utilised for other purposes if so required.

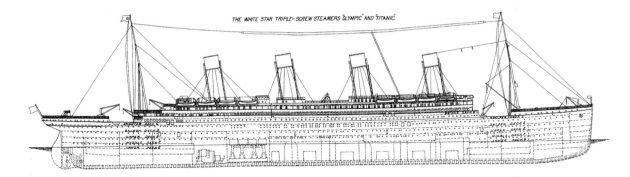

THE WHITE STAR TRIPLE–SCREW STEAMERS "OLYMPIC" AND "TITANIC".

Referring to other detailed drawings, shop managers, foremen, craftsmen, labourers and apprentices manufactured from steel, wood, copper, brass and glass the frames, plates, engines, boilers and thousands of other items that would, together, create the largest ships ever built.

Meticulously drawn and tinted plans were prepared for the ship's interior decor, showing panelling, classical columns, furniture, doors, window frames and the hundreds of other skillfully made items that were required to fit out a floating luxury hotel.

In 1906, during the early stages of the design, the White Star Line decided to move its express service from Liverpool to Southampton. As the *Mauretania* and *Lusitania* would be dominating the Merseyside port by the end of 1907, it was considered that Southampton not only had the advantage of being without a sand bar across its entrance (unlike the Mersey), but

The general arrangement of the Olympic-class ships. (Author's collection)

▲
The grand staircase, part of the luxury planned for First Class. (Titanic International)

'I cannot imagine any condition which would cause a ship to founder. I cannot conceive of any vital disaster happening to this vessel. Modern shipbuilding has gone beyond all that.'

Captain E.J. Smith on the maiden voyage of an earlier White Star liner, *Adriatic*, 1907

also had the phenomena of a double high tide, making the port accessible for longer periods.

The south coast port was nearer to London and better located for White Star to take advantage of the European and Near Eastern emigrant traffic that had, so far, been well-served by German, French and other shipping lines from continental ports.

The relocated White Star vessels would call at Cherbourg for continental traffic. The line's Liverpool-based ships would still take Irish and Scandinavian emigrants as before and Queenstown, in Ireland, would be used on both routes.

As part of new engineering facilities in Southampton Docks, Harland and Wolff built workshops and a dry dock (although this would not be big enough for the planned ships which would have to return to Belfast for dry-docking). A vast new wet dock that could berth the new super liners was built by the London and South Western Railway, the dock estate owners.

To test the Southampton facilities, and to open the line's new service, the *Adriatic* arrived at the end of her Liverpool to New York maiden voyage. On 22 May 1907 – the fifth anniversary of the acquisition of the White Star Line by the IMM – *Adriatic* sailed on the line's inaugural voyage from a jubilant Southampton. At 24,541gt, then the largest liner in the world, *Adriatic* had immediately doubled the size of ships previously handled by the port.

The scene was set for the new service to be run by *Olympic* and *Titanic* and the 12-year-old *Oceanic*. The way was clear to provide a weekly sailing from Southampton.

Both Southampton and White Star were delighted by their mutual good fortune.

◄
Titanic awaits embarking passengers at Cherbourg, just before dusk. (Private collection)

In 1907 Bram Stoker (author of the Gothic horror story, *Dracula*) wrote of Harland and Wolff's Belfast shipyard: 'It would be difficult to imagine any better object-lesson . . . from the point of view of commercial enterprise, than the magnitude, stability and prosperity of Harland and Wolff's shipbuilding yards . . . at the south end . . .

➤
As noted by the author Bram Stoker, three slipways at the Belfast shipyard were conjoined and, over these, a huge gantry, 840ft long and 250ft wide, was erected. (Ulster Folk & Transport Museum)

has lately been erected a . . . large gantry . . . wide enough to cover two great ships.'

While Stoker was penning his classic, an American author, Morgan Robertson, wrote a novel, *Futility*, about the sinking of a superliner. In the 1890s there had been concerned debate in Great Britain that legislation lagged behind advances in shipbuilding. Prominent men, such as publisher and writer W.T. Stead and Member of Parliament Admiral Lord Charles Beresford, assessed that it would only be a matter of time before an appalling accident would occur.

Contemporary Board of Trade legislation stipulated that a ship over 10,000gt should carry sixteen lifeboats (calculated *not* on the number of passengers). Although tonnages were rapidly increasing, the number of lifeboats did not.

Robertson's book took up this theme: his fictional ship was 40,000gt (four times larger than any contemporary ship), had inadequate lifeboat capacity for its 3,000 passengers, struck an iceberg and sank with a resultant heavy loss of life.

The name of Robertson's fictional liner was *Titan*.

In March 1912, Axel Welin read a learned paper before the Institution of Naval Architects. Using the latest White Star giants as a reference, Welin's new double-acting type of luffing davit could launch several lifeboats in quick succession: 'On the boat deck of . . . *Olympic*, and . . . *Titanic*, this double-acting type of davit has been fitted . . . in view of coming changes in official regulations . . . considered wise by the owners that these changes should be . . . anticipated, and . . . [would] make it possible to double,

◄
W.T. Stead, the great British editor and reformer and personal friend of the ship's original Chief Naval Architect, Alexander Carlisle, had written an article in the Pall Mall Gazette *in 1886 deploring the lack of lifeboats on ocean liners. He would later be a passenger on* Titanic. (Author's collection)

Did you know?
Titanic and *Olympic* were fitted with more than the officially required number of lifeboats.

The anticipated changes remained just that – anticipated. Neither the builders nor the owners wanted to expensively jump the legislative gun.

The ships had been designed to take up to sixty-two lifeboats and when the numbers were reduced so that promenading passengers could have an uninterrupted sea-vista, designer Alexander Carlisle was incensed. His subsequent resignation was accepted by his brother-in-law, Lord Pirrie, whose nephew, Thomas Andrews, then took over as design manager.

The legal requirements were 'exceeded' by the addition of four collapsibles: rigid-bottomed boats with canvas sides, stowed atop deck houses. Built to a high standard of compartmentisation, the Olympic-class liners would be able to float with at least two of their watertight compartments open to the

or even treble, the number of boats without any structural alterations, should such an increase prove to be necessary . . .'

sea, maybe even three or four. In effect, the 'very complete' subdivision of the ships was said to make them their own lifeboat.

Fifteen transverse bulkheads, also to current regulations, divided the liners into sixteen watertight compartments and were fitted with vertically operating watertight doors. These could be closed, as the souvenir edition of *The Shipbuilder* said, by 'simply moving an electric switch, [which would] instantly close the doors throughout and make the vessel practically unsinkable'. The qualifying 'practically' was omitted by the press.

The first keel plates of the primary ship of the class, the *Olympic* – Yard Number 400 – were laid down on 16 December, 1908. It would be on the building and progress of this first vessel that both press and public attention would be focused. At 120ft

longer than her Cunard rivals and with a 50 per cent increase on their tonnages, the new ship would be a sensation.

By March's end, building had progressed to *Olympic*'s tank tops. On Wednesday

▼
The Titanic *under construction.* (Ulster Folk & Transport Museum)

➤
Framework surrounds the Titanic *(left) and* Olympic *(right) for the construction of the sides and decks.* (Ulster Folk & Transport Museum)

31 March 1909, the first keel plates of the second ship, Yard Number 401, were laid on the adjoining slipway. This ship would be *Titanic*.

Already the public were keenly looking forward to the advent of the new giants. A statement placed over advertisements for the line's various services to the United States, Canada and Australia read: 'ROYAL MAIL STEAMERS: OLYMPIC, 45,000 TONS AND TITANIC, 45,000 TONS. LARGEST STEAMERS IN THE WORLD BUILDING.'

As the tank tops of *Olympic* were completed and plated over, so elegantly shaped frames were erected, the last of which, specially painted, was raised on 20 November 1909.

The liner entered the River Lagan on 20 October 1910, amid great jubilation but without ceremony. It was White Star's

policy not to subscribe to formal launches, satisfied that the event was witnessed and celebrated by the attendance of special guests and ticketed spectators. As one shipyard worker dourly observed: 'They just builds 'em and chucks 'em in!'

Many proudly witnessed the liner being launched, particularly Lord Pirrie whose

shipyard had designed and built her, J. Bruce Ismay, for whose company she had been built, and J. Pierpont Morgan whose financial combine (along with the remortgaging of existing ships) had enabled the largest liner in the world to come into being. They must have earnestly congratulated themselves.

Work progressed steadily on *Titanic* while her sister lay alongside the fitting-out wharf. A massive floating crane lifted boilers on board *Olympic* as her structure reached completion and her interiors were decorated: luxury in First Class and elegant comfort in Second.

Fore and aft spaces were readied for what would comprise the majority of her future passengers. Ordinary Third-Class passengers would find their accommodation, although seemingly basic, pleasant enough. To those escaping poverty the ship would offer unimaginable luxury.

Many emigrants would be leaving rude, earthen-floored dwellings, candles or lanterns and no running water or sanitation (the use of the latter facilities often being taught by the ship's stewards who would

▲
The launching of Olympic, 20 October 1910. (Ulster Folk & Transport Museum)

rather not be clearing up after untrained wards). The serving of three regular meals a day on tables covered with linen would be a luxury not dreamed of in the homes left behind by the emigrants in their adventure to reach the New World.

Wednesday 31 May 1911, and Belfast was once again *en fête*. Not only was the brand new *Olympic* ready to leave for her port of registration, Liverpool, but she was proudly being put on show after completing two days of successful sea trials. The local population had the chance to inspect her with the resultant receipts given to hospitals in Belfast.

A few days previously, the North Atlantic had given White Star's pride and joy, the elegantly beautiful *Oceanic,* a salutary demonstration of her power. Westward-bound from Daunt's Rock, *Oceanic*

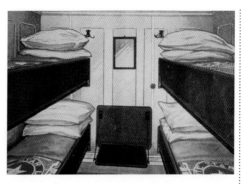

◄
A Third-Class cabin, typified by white enamelled steel deckheads and wooden panelled bulkheads. (Titanic International)

had encountered heavy seas which accompanied her across the Atlantic until, on 21 March, she encountered a heavy squall. A jolt was felt as lightning struck her foremast, the top wooden 9ft of which fell to the deck, bringing down wireless aerials but fortunately missing the saloon's ornate glass. Railings were damaged in its fall and First Officer Lightoller narrowly avoided serious injury. Commendably, the 'Queen

◄◄
Alongside Olympic's *vacated slipway,* Titanic *stands on the ways a few weeks from her own launch.* (Ulster Folk & Transport Museum)

23

of the Sea' still arrived in New York on time. But now, prior to the *Olympic*'s departure later that bright, blustery May day, those who had inspected the ship and those who had come as guests for the inaugural crossing were also in the shipyard to witness another momentous event: the launching of her sistership, *Titanic*.

Stands had been erected for those who possessed a ticket enabling them to view the launch from within the yard. Thousands more assembled outside. An estimated 100,000 people had come to follow *Titanic* as she entered her natural element for the first time.

Special guests arrived from England on the ferry *Duke of Argyll*, including J. Pierpont Morgan. He and Lord Pirrie had reserved suites for the *Titanic*'s maiden voyage scheduled for mid-March 1912.

Among the spectators were James MacQuitty, managing director of W&G Baird, proprietors of the *Belfast Telegraph*, and his son, William, who had over the previous few weeks excitedly asked how such an enormous ship could be launched into the sea. James had patiently explained that it would take over 20 tons of tallow, train oil and soft soap spread over the launching ways to enable the ship's huge hull to slide down the gradual slope to the river before the land lost its grip on her for ever.

Signal flags spelling 'Success', along with British, American and White Star Line flags, flew from atop the Arrol gantry. Young William recalled eighty years later: 'At five minutes past noon, a red flag was hoisted to warn the fleet of boats in the River Lagan to stand clear. Another five minutes went by before a rocket was fired

and workers began to hammer at the restraining chocks. At 12.13 (two minutes earlier than scheduled) the firing of a second rocket reduced the vast crowd to silence. Would this huge vessel ever move? All at once the workers on board gave a cheer in which the crowds on shore joined. The slide had begun. Every ship in the lough sounded its siren, the noise drowning the roar of the piles of restraining anchors

The launch of Titanic *on 31 May 1911 took 62 seconds.* (Ulster Folk & Transport Museum)

as they were dragged along the ground. Slowly gathering speed, the *Titanic* moved smoothly down the ways, and a minute later was plunging into the water and raising a huge wave. I felt a great lump in my throat and an enormous pride in being an Ulsterman.'

The invited guests boarded the *Olympic*, gaily bedecked with flags. Following the spectacle and a crossing of the North Channel the liner anchored in the River Mersey and, after her guests had disembarked, boatloads of visitors arrived to tour her, each paying 2s 6d – half-a-crown – for the privilege. The receipts again went to local hospitals. At midnight, the *Olympic* weighed anchor and headed south.

Twice the size of anything else that the citizens of Southampton had seen, the *Olympic* created a sensation and

A flag-bedecked Olympic on show at Liverpool, 1911. (Stewart Bale/ Author's collection)

was civically received by the Mayor of Southampton, Colonel Bance, who was also Admiral of the Port and Chairman of the Harbour Board.

Olympic moored alongside Berths 44–45 in the new deep-water White Star dock, purposely constructed on the old Oyster Bay for the new 'Queens of the Seas'. A parallelogram in shape, the dock was 1,000ft long, 400ft wide and covered 16 acres to a depth of 40ft at low water and 53ft at high.

The next eleven days were spent in storing and readying the ship for her passengers.

On 8 June Lord Pirrie and Harold Sanderson, General Manager of the White Star Line, attended a special lunch on

> '*Olympic* **is a marvel, and has given unbounded satisfaction.**'
>
> Bruce Ismay, Chairman of the White Star Line.

➤
Southampton was delighted to receive Olympic *on 3 June 1911.* (Author's collection)

board. The advent of the new liner was being widely fêted with a great deal of welcomed publicity.

At midday on 14 June 1911, amid a further welter of publicity and in an atmosphere of great excitement, the *Olympic* was pulled away from the dockside by tugs of the Southampton, Isle of Wight and South of England Royal Mail Steam Packet Company, and her bow turned downstream into Southampton Water.

The great adventure had begun.

The new *Olympic* sailed through the English Channel on the short journey to Cherbourg and then on to Queenstown. From there it was transatlantic all the way to New York where a fantastic welcome awaited her – the world's largest liner in the world's most thriving metropolis.

The maiden voyage was all that IMM, the White Star Line and Bruce Ismay could have desired and Ismay subsequently telegraphed Lord Pirrie, praising the *Olympic*: 'My warmest and most sincere congratulations. Will cable you full particulars [regarding] speed, consumption [of coal] later.'

There was an initial disappointment with the inefficient operation of the two Cherbourg passenger and baggage tenders when *Olympic* made her maiden call there. *Nomadic* (1911, 1,273gt) and *Traffic* (1911, 675gt) had been specially built to service the new liners, replacing the *Gallic*, an ex-Birkenhead Corporation paddle ferry.

Nevertheless, so delighted was Ismay with the liner that during this trip a firm decision was made to build a third ship of the class. Even the advance publicity for the first two ships made no mention of a third vessel which would have made excellent copy had she been planned. The contract for this third ship, *Gigantic* (later renamed *Britannic*), was placed a few weeks after Ismay's decision.

The chairman's observations during the maiden trip indicated his overall pleasure at the *Olympic*'s performance: the over-springiness of mattresses which 'accentuated the pulsation of the ship' (beds were *too* comfortable!) and the lack of cigar and cigarette holders in the toilets were indicative of his attention to detail.

Did you know?
The swimming pool was filled with heated salt water and First-Class passengers paid 4s for its use. This was equivalent to 6 hours' labour for a working-class man.

A luxuriously appointed First-Class cabin complete with eiderdown on the bed. (Ulster Folk & Transport Museum)

suites, two of which even had private promenades, would give the second sister the epithet of being the most luxurious liner in the world as well as the largest. External windows would be reconfigured as a result. An outward extension of the exclusive à la carte restaurant (where First-Class passengers could dine on the payment of a supplement) was also suggested, while an equal space to starboard was transformed into the Café Parisien.

Another modification included on *Titanic* during her building was the glazing of the forward part of Promenade Deck A; a late alteration incorporated after a particularly rough return crossing of *Olympic* when she proved to be a wet ship in that area.

He also recommended that the outside cabins on Bridge Deck B be extended to the ship's side to utilise under-used promenade space. This feature would be built into *Titanic* and the resultant

Unlike the *Lusitania* and *Mauretania*, the Olympic-class vessels were intended to be identical both internally and externally, but

◀
The Café Parisien adjoining the à la carte restaurant. (Ulster Folk & Transport Museum)

The Titanic's fourth dummy funnel was the last to be erected. A- and B-deck modifications have yet to be undertaken. (Ulster Folk & Transport Museum)

the alterations provided a distinct external distinguishing feature between the two sisters.

Titanic took on fittings that had been similarly installed in her senior sister: engines, boilers, fans, auxiliary machinery, propellers, steering gear, ovens, condensers, evaporators, panelling, chairs, carpets, paintings, palms, lifts, furnishings – all of which made multiple production economically sound. A swimming pool (one of the first afloat), tiles for a Turkish bath and 10,000 other items that were required to regale an ocean liner could be manufactured without a change of tooling or materials.

Even the internal decor drawings that had been used for *Olympic* were recycled for *Titanic*, as were some of the photographs taken of the *Olympic* during her construction and fitting-out.

The Belfast photographer, R. Welch, took dozens of excellent pictures of the 'senior' ship but only a few of *Titanic* herself.

The early good fortune of the *Olympic* was not to hold and she was soon to receive a disastrous setback.

Even as *Olympic* arrived in New York the unexpected mass of her bulk caused a tug

The two huge sets of reciprocating engines that would drive the Titanic's outer propellers. (Ulster Folk & Transport Museum)

33

to break away from its moorings, resulting in a collision. The liner was unharmed but the tug's owners claimed damages.

Three months later, on 20 September, and about an hour after sailing, the *Olympic*, still under the command of Captain Edward J. Smith, had reached the point in The Solent where, after leaving the mouth of Southampton Water, she made a turn to starboard. A turn to port then completed a tricky reverse 'S' manoeuvre to navigate an awkward channel between the Brambles and Thorn sandbanks.

At the same time, steaming eastwards from the Needles, Captain William Blunt of the Royal Navy's cruiser, HMS *Hawke*, made an assumption that the big liner was heading eastwards at a constant speed. The *Olympic*'s speed, however, was steadily increasing as she straightened from her manoeuvre. *Hawke* tried to overtake before realising the liner's intentions.

The cruiser attempted to drop astern of the liner and go aft about her, but her helm did not respond. With the grating of steel against steel, *Hawke* crashed into the liner's starboard side, her ram bow opening a V-shaped gash just beneath *Olympic*'s Poop Deck, about 90ft from her sternpost.

Dining passengers were treated to a pall of smoke (presumably from the *Hawke*) entering the saloon through an open door. Some passengers complained of nausea; others speculated collision with a rock, or even a whale.

Olympic anchored in Osborne Bay; the cruiser limped towards Portsmouth's Royal Naval Dockyard where, after a telephone call had been taken by a passing yard boy, a dry dock was hastily prepared to receive

the warship whose badly crumpled ram had by then fallen off.

After an overnight anchorage off the Isle of Wight, the liner, with the assistance of six tugs, took 2½ hours to return to Southampton. The *Olympic* was declared a wreck and her crew's wages were stopped – a lamentable practice that would continue until well into the Second World War.

Two special trains were chartered to take mail and passengers who wished to find alternative berths on other of the company's ships sailing that week from Liverpool or on the *Noordam* from Boulogne in France. Those preferring to stay in Southampton were found accommodation and other berths.

One passenger, Mr Sheldon, hired a special train to Liverpool at a cost of £78 in order to catch the *Adriatic*. Fortunately the ship was 10 minutes late in sailing and Sheldon caught it with just minutes to spare.

A substantial wooden-planked patch was fitted to make the *Olympic*'s damage sufficiently seaworthy. She sailed for Belfast on 3 October for full repairs, making about 10 knots during the three-day voyage.

Olympic was initially held responsible for the accident but, after subsequent tank tests at Teddington, the blame was equally apportioned. The little-understood

'I never saw a wreck. I have never been wrecked. I have never been in a predicament that threatened to end in disaster.'

Captain E.J. Smith in a press interview, 1907.

phenomenon of 'shallow water or 'canal effect' was cited as the cause.

Titanic was removed from dry dock and men taken from her to work on her injured sister. Items intended for the second ship were transferred to *Olympic* to hasten her repair and return her to service. Badly chipped propeller blades also had to be replaced.

The urgent need to get *Olympic* back into service postponed Ismay's hoped-for alterations to her layout for the foreseeable future.

By this time, the Olympic-class claim to be the 'largest in the world' was under threat as Cunard had ordered *Aquitania* (45,700gt) and Germany's Hamburg-America Line had two 50,000 tonners planned, *Imperator* and *Europa* (later renamed *Vaterland*). As a response, the newspaper *The Scotsman*, rumoured that 'the White Star Line contemplates . . . a contract for a steamer 992 feet in length'.

A further statement announced that the keel of a White Star liner, with a length of 1,000ft and which would 'eclipse in size and . . . luxuriousness . . . the *Olympic* and *Titanic*' had been laid, adding that the new ship would have a 'cricket field, golf links . . . tennis courts, plunge and other . . . baths, gymnasium [and] shops . . .' This could have been corporate posturing as the *Gigantic*'s build commenced.

On 20 November, after six weeks of repairs, *Olympic* left Belfast and work

recommenced on *Titanic*. It had been officially announced back in early October that, because of the delays, *Titanic*'s

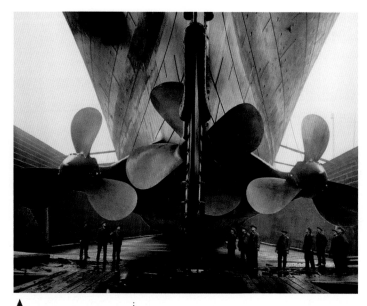

▲
All three propellers as fitted to Olympic *as shown were similarly fitted to* Titanic. (Author's collection)

maiden voyage would take place later than intended. Originally proposed for 20 March 1912, it was now rescheduled for 10 April.

On 3 February 1912, she returned to dry dock for a fortnight.

The following month saw *Titanic* alongside the fitting-out wharf, with work under way on A-deck's glazed windows. *Olympic* returned once again to the Thompson Graving Dock, this time for repairs to a propeller which had lost a blade during a westbound crossing on 24 February. This would probably be the last time that the two sisters would meet.

Unbeknown to the British public, the Golden Age – the Belle Epoch – of the late 'Edwardian Summer' was coming to an end as political tensions rose in Europe. The British Empire had a new king, but Great Britain had been going through a turbulent time and industrial troubles in early 1912 were creating difficulties for the smooth running of the nation.

Across the Atlantic, America was having its share of unrest: between 1910 and 1911, coal miners had struck for a better standard of wages. About 15,000 miners were affected and by the end of the strike sixteen of them had been killed.

The desire to improve wages crossed the Western Ocean and the Welsh miners also struggled for a fair minimum wage. This would soon have an impact on the whole country. By January 1912 the miners' actions had escalated and the Miners' Federation of Great Britain balloted its members. A vote was taken and a national coal strike commenced at the end of February.

By early March the strike had brought much of the nation's trade and industry to

▼
Olympic *(right) is ready to sail again, 6 March 1912.* (Harland and Wolff)

Did you know?
Titanic's hull contained 3 million rivets fastened either by hand or by a hydraulic press.

a halt. Inevitably this caused hardship to the working population who, in the days when coal was king, found themselves out of work and reliant on the common good and Salvation Army soup kitchens. Coal shortages caused disruption to train timetables and many merchant steamships found themselves laid up idle with empty bunkers.

In spite of the strike, White Star announced that services would be maintained, although the speed of the 23-knot *Olympic* – and soon that of *Titanic* – would be reduced to 20 knots, 'to husband . . . resources'. Sailings would be 'ensured . . . throughout the season'.

By 25 March the coal strike had lost much of its impetus and, a week later, despite the miners' continued dissatisfaction, they gradually returned to work.

The upper deck of Titanic. (Author's collection)

Did you know?

The Olympic-class helm orders were the old sailing ship tiller orders. Hence a turn to port would require the helm to be put to starboard.

In Belfast *Titanic* had been bunkered with 3,000 tons of coal in readiness for her trials on Monday 1 April. Some of the bunkers began to smoulder and would not be extinguished until the 13th.

Complete apart from its final storing, the liner's command had been given to Edward J. Smith ('E.J.'), White Star's senior captain, and he would take *Titanic* on her maiden voyage as he had done with many of

Titanic *prepares to sail.*
(Author's collection)

the company's ships, having recently been transferred from the *Olympic*. Command of the latter ship had been assumed by the appropriately named Captain Haddock who had stood by *Titanic* during her final stages of building.

E.J., reputedly the highest paid skipper on the lucrative North Atlantic, earned around £1,200 per annum plus a handsome bonus for safe navigation. With such a bonus at stake he, along with his chosen officers, would not be one to take chances with a ship under his command, unless they were well-judged and seasoned decisions, made with the advantage of years of experience.

Transferring from other White Star ships, his officers, a fine, experienced group, joined the *Titanic* in Belfast to acquaint themselves with the ship they would sail on her delivery trip. William Murdoch was appointed Chief

Officer; Charles Herbert Lightoller, First Officer; David Blair, Second; Herbert Pitman, Third; Joseph Boxhall, Fourth; Harold Lowe, Fifth; and James Moody, Sixth.

For the short trip south, a temporary crew also signed on under 'Coastal Articles'. A crew for the maiden voyage would be appointed in Hampshire.

It was anticipated that the *Titanic* would, as had her sister, make a courtesy visit to Liverpool for public inspection before sailing for southern waters. However, high winds on 1 April precluded the new ship from leaving Belfast for sea trials. It was not until the following day that the weather abated and the ship, under the care of tugs, was able to leave her quay in the Abercorn Basin at 6 a.m.

With her outer propellers in motion, she steamed into the North Channel, her

Titanic is carefully tended by her entourage of tugs. (Illustrated London News, 20 April 1912)

engines now powering her propellers as, with smoke vigorously pouring into the breeze from her forward three funnels, she glided across the calm waters. The delayed debut meant that the ship's Liverpool call was cancelled, and Captain Smith would

join the ship in Southampton where he had been celebrating his daughter's 14th birthday.

At sea at last with all three propellers under full power, *Titanic* underwent 10 hours of trials. Prolonged testing of her abilities was probably not deemed necessary as sufficient data had been obtained from the *Olympic*, whose thorough trials had taken two days to complete, achieving 21¾ knots, ¾ of a knot faster than her contracted speed.

> 'Should an accident occur through which a [*passenger*] **vessel . . . goes quickly to the bottom, the loss of life would be appauling** [*sic*].'
>
> Fourth Officer Geoffrey Barnish of the *Carpathia*.

Nevertheless, *Titanic* still underwent specific trials, including turning circles to test her manoeuvrability (she could make a complete turn in just over four times her own length) and an emergency stop: 20 knots to standing dead in the water in about half a mile.

At around 7 p.m. she returned to Belfast. Her anchors were tested to the Board of Trade representative's satisfaction, who then signed a certificate of seaworthiness, valid for one year.

Those of the trials team, apart from the Guarantee Group and essential workmen who had not signed 'Coastal Articles', were disembarked. *Titanic* turned and, once more, headed out to sea, a course set southwards for her next stop: Southampton.

◀◀
Titanic *sailing down Belfast Lough.* (Ulster Folk & Transport Museum)

After a brief, mist-encountered coastal voyage, the new liner docked in her designated home port just after midnight on Wednesday 3 April, two days before Easter.

A Southampton newspaper wrote a report that accentuated the absence of the fanfare that had greeted *Olympic*'s arrival: 'Quietly and unostentatiously, without any blare of trumpets, the *Titanic*, the world's latest and biggest ship, steamed up the silent waters of the Solent and docked . . . at midnight, taking the same berth in the new wet dock that the *Olympic* had occupied 12 hours before.'

The coastal crew signed off, some pocketing a few illicit 'souvenirs' as they disembarked. A sea-going crew in the three departments of Deck, Victualling and Engineering then signed Articles between 6 and 8 April, with local halls being used for the purpose. Nearly 700 out of almost 900 crew gave Southampton addresses.

After signing on, two brothers, Samuel and Alfred Pugh, chanced to meet. On hearing that a third brother, Percy, had also joined, Sam fumed that it was 'unlucky to have three brothers on . . . the same ship', and walked off. Alfred and Percy sailed with the ship, the former as a steward, the other a leading fireman.

Using *Olympic* notepaper with 'Titanic – don't forget' written over the heading, Bedroom Steward George Beedem told his mother and family that he had been transferred from the *Olympic* to the *Titanic*. By Good Friday, Beedem was feeling rather despondent as most of the crew had left for the holidays. But he and a dozen others remained on board, apparently unpaid. He

Titanic

On board R.M.S. ——

dont forget

Dear Mother.

I have done two days got back Thursday morning you can hardly tell the difference between the two boats. I've been standing the ship to day to see she doesn't run away. nobody his been ... doing ... being Good Friday so I lose a days pay ... so come. Mc.B keeps me in work

some fool leaving us the list I am sending 10/- thats if short so I've managed to exsist on about 8/- counting if I had from you so its a happy life. I have no news to tell you only the last 3 days I've left rotten + what with no ... or anything to work with. I wish the belly ship at the bottom of the sea. I heard from Mother to day Uncle John is a little

◄

In these extracts from Steward George Beedam's letters home (to his mother, left, and 'Nell and Charlie', right) he airs his frustrations on being transferred to Titanic. (Private collection)

47

aired his frustrations, writing to 'Nell and Charlie' to say that he had been suffering from a cold since the last call of *Olympic* into Plymouth.

Beedem was not alone in his dissatisfaction: the captain's steward, Arthur Paintin, later wrote to his parents from Queenstown, comparing the *Titanic* to the *Olympic*: '. . . what a fine ship this [is], much better than the *Olympic* as far as the passengers are concerned . . . but my little room is nothing near so nice, no daylight, electric light on all day.' He added: 'I suppose it's no use grumbling.'

Frustration also existed among the officers. Captain Smith wanted a senior officer with him who had experience with the *Olympic*, so Henry Wilde was transferred to *Titanic* as Chief Officer, probably in preparation for eventual command.

William Murdoch, a very experienced and ambitious Scot, replaced Charles Lightoller as First Officer and Lightoller reverted to Second. Second Officer David Blair left the ship with the words: 'This is a magnificent ship, I feel very disappointed.' The junior officers retained their ranks.

As the White Star Line prepared its ship for the voyage, in a salute to the people of Southampton, *Titanic* was dressed overall with bunting which fluttered gaily on that pleasant, sunny Easter holiday.

For many of the seamen who lived in the city, Easter 1912 was a memorable holiday because, having been without jobs for the long weeks of the coal strike, the coming of the *Titanic* meant a return to work. Also, as a result of the holiday, storing and finishing had been delayed so few visitors were permitted access to the ship. Hundreds of items had to be taken on board including a consignment of tableware which comprised fine Spode bone china with a cobalt blue design, destined for the à la carte restaurant.

Among the privileged few who were allowed access during this busy time were journalists and a journal illustrator, renowned artist Norman Wilkinson. (Fellow artist and illustrator Charles Dixon had

On Good Friday 1912 in Southampton the flags were flying on Titanic. (Author's collection)

recently completed a painting depicting *Titanic* as she lay alongside her Belfast fitting-out berth at night with an uncannily prescient atmosphere.)

Wilkinson would later write: 'I saw the new White Star liner "Titanic". She was to sail on her maiden voyage that afternoon.' The artist also knew the captain: '. . . nearly sixty years old, with forty years service [he] radiated Edwardian confidence . . . a warm welcome, but [was] extremely busy.'

Wilkinson observed his own painting, *Entrance to Plymouth Harbour*, hanging over the mantelpiece in the smoking room. This room was a superb compartment panelled in mahogany and lavishly inlaid with designs in mother-of-pearl, where gentlemen would retire to indulge in after-dinner cigars. A companion piece, *Entrance to New York Harbour*, hung, similarly situated, on the *Olympic*.

Another feature of this masculine-orientated room was the stained-glass windows, illuminated from the concealed side, which hid the uptake of the fourth funnel so that light infiltrated the compartment from all directions.

Wilkinson's 'splendid ship' was also looking her best to casual observers from the shore, or as they passed by the dock to and from the Isle of Wight.

To freshen the great lady's make-up, workmen had sat spider-like on trapezes as they repainted the four huge black-topped funnels rising above the white superstructure surmounting the black hull. A 9in gold band separated the hull from the white mountain above it. The simple elegance of *Titanic*'s Edwardian design belied her great size.

Design manager Thomas Andrews, staying at the South Western Hotel, a mere 10 minutes walk away from the dockside, made daily tours of 'his' ship with the Guarantee Group, comprised of technical and trade

◄◄
Norman Wilkinson's early concept painting of Titanic *(showing her with only one mast) shows her dressed from the foremast in an imaginative setting.* (Author's collection)

Did you know?
There were forty-eight millionaires on board *Titanic*.

◄
The stained glass of the Smoking Room concealed the uptake to the fourth funnel, used as a vent. (Ulster Folk & Transport Museum)

Several passengers from the laid-up liners were reassigned to *Titanic* and most were delighted at the 'upgrade' to the world's largest, newest and most luxurious liner; all except for Mrs Esther Hart. Her husband, Benjamin, and daughter, Eva, were thrilled by the new arrangement but, full of foreboding, Esther was unhappy about being on such a big ship. She would spend the next few nights fully dressed, while sleeping during the day.

The crew began to arrive just after dawn on 10 April for muster. Some of the men returned ashore where, seamen being seamen and not yet required for duty, they headed towards one or more of the local public houses in the locality: The Grapes, The Old Oriental, The Newcastle Hotel. Drink was not allowed on board to the crew, so they took it to the ship themselves.

staff from the shipyard, noting those details that required immediate or future attention.

Coaling still needed to be completed and quantities were transferred from laid-up IMM vessels – *Philadelphia*, *Majestic*, *New York* and *Oceanic* – to enable their larger sister to sail. A total of 6,000 tons would eventually fill *Titanic*'s bunkers.

➤
Alfred Slade, one of three brothers who were entered on Titanic's log book *as 'deserters'. (By kind permission of Mark Slade & family)*

➤➤
Third-Class passengers on the Poop Deck at Queenstown. (Author's collection)

Another band of brothers, the Slades (Thomas, Bertram and Alfred), also went ashore with their work-mates, visiting a couple of the nearby hostelries.

Meanwhile, the passengers had begun to arrive.

The first to board the ship were Third-Class passengers: the poor, the impecunious, the emigrants who were fleeing their old countries with their whole world packed into meagre suitcases, like millions had before and millions would after them. They were going to a Land of the Free ('Give me your tired, your poor. . . . The wretched refuse of your teeming shore. . . . Send these, the homeless, tempest-tossed, to me'*), a land that did not really want them.

Not all Third-Class passengers were fleeing their pasts. Thirty-year-old bricklayer Charles Warren was going ahead of his wife and five children to establish himself

*First-Class passenger, Isidor Straus, co-founder of Macy's department store in New York.
(Author's collection)*

*Taken from the quotation found at the base of the Statue of Liberty.

before sending for those whom he had left behind.

Third-Class passengers formed a queue on the dockside, snaking slowly along towards the medical officials who inspected them for signs of disease, such as glaucoma, that would prohibit their entry into the New World. Once cleared they entered the ship via the Third-Class gangway on 'E'-Deck. (A similar inspection would face them on arrival in New York.)

A boat train carrying Second- and Third-Class passengers arrived from London at around 9.30 a.m., followed 2 hours later by another, this one carrying First-Class passengers. By arriving later, the privileged, gilded set would not have to wait or mingle with those of the 'lower orders'.

Among the First-Class passengers was W.T. Stead, who was visiting the United States at the invitation of President Taft to address a peace conference at Carnegie Hall. Also arriving were Mr and Mrs Isidor Straus, and Lucy Noël Martha, Countess of Rothes, who was going to Canada to join her husband in celebration of their twelfth wedding anniversary.

In the nearby pubs the crew members looked at the clocks and realised they had better return to the ship. The Slade brothers followed their companions into the docks. A train was rattling by and the Slades waited for it to pass. By the time they reached the ship's side the crew's gangway was being lifted and the attendant officer refused to allow them to board.

They had to return home. Not only were the men still without a job but they were

Sam Williams, who left an illegitimate son, 'Little Sam', in the city. Neither the child nor his mother have ever been traced. (Courtesy of Ron Williams)

also without the few pennies they had had in their pockets, and the aroma of beer was still about them.

One day preceding the sailing, young fireman Sam Williams left The Old Oriental with some shipmates. Cautioned by a policeman at the dock gate for boisterous behaviour, Sam ill-advisedly struck the officer and then, when he realised the seriousness of his actions, ran away to his Uncle Ted's house in Lower Canal Walk. Ted gave him his own Discharge Book for Sam to sign on the 'unsinkable' ship. Young Williams thus returned to the ship under an alias.

Smoke rolled from the ship's forward three funnels as tugs busied themselves around the black steel cliff that towered over them. Groups of well-wishers on the quayside exchanged farewells with passengers lining the ship's rails. Others on board either busied themselves settling into their cabins or explored the new wonder that would be their home for the next seven days.

Captain Steele, White Star's Marine Superintendent, sat on a baulk of timber watching the events with an expert's eye as *Titanic* pulled away from her berth.

A maiden voyage had begun.

'God Himself could not sink this ship!'

Quote from the dockside to a passenger.

White Star's Marine Superintendent in Southampton, Captain Steele (foreground), watches Titanic's *departure, 10 April 1912. (Author's collection)*

It was midday on Wednesday 10 April 1912 as the thick moorings and springs holding the *Titanic* to the cast-iron bollards along the dock's edge were cast off and the great ship was gently coerced into the expansive waters of the White Star dock by her attendant tugs, *Albert Edward, Ajax, Hector, Hercules, Neptune* and *Vulcan*.

Once clear of her berth, *Titanic*'s propellers (probably just the outers which could be used to assist manoeuvring) started their work. Gently the liner moved ahead into the River Test. Her bow was then turned almost 90 degrees to port; ahead lay Southampton Water and, 12 miles to the south, The Solent.

Three IMM ships (American Line's *St Louis, Philadelphia* and White Star's 1891 Blue Riband holder, *Majestic)* were laid-up opposite *Titanic*'s now-vacated berth.

A few hundred yards downstream, two more ships were berthed in tandem. White Star's previous darling, the *Oceanic*, was against Berths 34–35 and, outside of her, was the *New York* (ex-Inman liner *City of New York* and 1893 record holder), also of the American Line.

Titanic's puffing consort of tugs, their work completed, headed back to await their next jobs as their recent charge progressed under her own power.

Only nine months previously, the biggest ship that The Solent had seen had been White Star's *Adriatic* of 24,451gt; before that, a ship of 10,000 tons (such as the *New York*) would have been worthy of remark. But now 46,000 tons was the upper norm and their operators were still becoming accustomed to handling these huge bulks.

➤
This heavily retouched picture of the Olympic *shows how* Titanic *would have appeared as she turned the dock's 'knuckle' into Southampton Water.* (Author's collection)

Titanic   Millvina Dean

New York *is edged between* Titanic *and* Oceanic *(left).*

Displacing a lot of water – 52,250 tons – *Titanic*'s draught left just a few feet between her keel and the river bed. As she passed the two liners to port, moored peacefully in tandem near the confluence of the rivers Test and Itchen, water rushed aft from her bow, trapped under pressure between her hull and the quays, before swiftly flowing round her stern.

Suddenly, 'there was a crack . . . then four more . . . like pistol shots in quick succession' as *New York*'s after lines parted, flying into the crowd who were following *Titanic*'s serene progress. The stern of the *New York*, caught by the flow of water, swung towards the passing after-quarter of *Titanic*. On her bridge, Captain Smith and Pilot George Bowyer assessed the situation and, with a hurried ringing of telegraph bells, the captain ordered the ship astern which had the effect of halting *Titanic*'s forward progress while slowly washing the *New York* away. The two ships had come to within just a few feet of a collision and, had one occurred, *Titanic* might have been compelled to return to her berth, or even to Belfast, thus delaying her departure. Recent memories of the *Olympic–Hawke* collision must have haunted the captain's mind.

With her forward motion arrested, *Titanic* drifted slightly astern as the *Vulcan* rushed up to put a line aboard the *New York* to pull her away to safety. Turned in front of *Titanic*, the maverick liner was taken to a berth on the Itchen quays.

Describing the near-miss, Arthur Paintin remarked in his letter home: 'There was great excitement . . . but I don't think there was any damage done bar one or two people knocked over by the ropes.'

The passengers were full of excitement: some not a little unworried. Thomas Andrews was especially concerned by the event: '. . . the situation was decidedly unpleasant.'

In penning a note to his son, Chief Engineer Joseph Bell said, 'no damage was done but it looked like trouble at the time'.

◄
Attempts being made to swing New York's *stern clear of the two ships.*

Did you know?
The bollards that *Titanic* moored against in the White Star dock in Southampton are still there today.

◄
New York's *stern, as seen ahead of* Titanic, *with Third-Class passengers observing the scene.*
(Fr Browne Collection/ Davison & Associates Ltd, Dublin)

After an hour *Titanic* got under way, only to slow again to allow some unneeded men to disembark onto *Vulcan* (a shell door had been opened in readiness), her work with the *New York* now completed.

▼
Titanic at a standstill having narrowly avoided an accident. Some spectators climb into railway wagons for a better view. (Author's collection)

Titanic's captain had cautiously ordered the starboard anchor to be lowered to within a few feet of the water, not to be re-stowed until well past the point off Cowes where *Olympic* had had her unfortunate encounter with HMS *Hawke*.

Titanic steamed on; past Hythe Pier to starboard with its little railway; past Netley Castle snuggling in the shoreside woods to port, followed by the quarter-mile Royal Victoria Hospital off which a Union Castle liner was laid-up at anchor.

As she progressed down Southampton Water, local photographers such as Stuart, Beken, Debenham and Hopkins, recorded

'I still don't like this ship. . . . I have a queer feeling about it.'

Chief Officer Henry Wilde.

her passing for posterity. Stuart took a splendid photograph of the liner as she passed a pleasure yacht under sail, the liner's hull plates highlighted by the sun.

Emerging from the confines of Southampton Water, with the wooded shores of the New Forest to starboard, the liner sailed past Calshot Spit with its castle built in the time of Henry VIII. Here she turned to starboard as she entered the waters of The Solent, passing the red-painted Calshot Spit lightvessel.

Meanwhile, the Royal Mail Steam Packet Company's *Tagus*, that had been overtaken by the ship in Southampton Water, crossed her wake and headed down the western Solent towards the Needles.

A little further on, the Thorn and Brambles channel was safely navigated while over to starboard could be seen the rented estate

◄
Titanic *passing Netley.*
(Author's collection)

◄
The Tagus *of the RMSP Co. passes astern. A lone figure walks on the deck of* Titanic, *probably not the captain, as is often thought.* (Fr Browne Collection/Davison & Associates Ltd, Dublin)

➤

Guglielmo Marconi, who would have been travelling on Titanic *with his family had he not cancelled due to an earlier appointment across the Atlantic.* (By kind permission of the Estate of Captain John Pritchard)

Did you know?
The 400,000 items of mail on board *Titanic* were sorted in the ship's Post Office by five postal clerks – two British and three American.

of Guglielmo Marconi, the developer of seagoing wireless.

Titanic carried two operators, 'Jack' Phillips and Harold Bride, and was fitted with one of the very latest, powerful wireless sets. Employed by the Marconi International Marine Communication Company and not by White Star, they would be busy during the voyage with messages sent to and from the wealthy set of passengers. Occasional official messages for the captain, especially those received with a coded prefix, were taken to the bridge.

After passing Marconi's house, Luttrell's Tower (aka Eaglehurst), the ship made one of two turns to port that brought her on to a course running parallel to Cowes and the northern shores of the Isle of Wight.

Passing East Cowes, the honey-coloured towers of Queen Victoria's summer palace,

Osborne House, rose above the verdant woods cascading down to the shore; past the uncompleted Quarr Abbey and through Spithead where several warships stood sentinel to the nearby Royal Dockyard at Portsmouth. The ship again slowed to allow George Bowyer to disembark into a pilots' sailing vessel before again picking up speed to sail through 'Palmerston's Follies' – three forts straddling Spithead between the island and the mainland. Entering the English Channel she passed

A photograph taken by Marconi's wife and daughter, who then rushed to the top of Luttrell's Tower as Titanic *sailed by.* (Courtesy of the University of Liverpool)

the Nab lightvessel before a course was set for the French port of Cherbourg.

It was a pleasant, if chilly, day as passengers promenaded the Boat Deck, taking in the Channel air. Others wrote letters home that would be taken ashore in Queenstown, her last port of call before setting off across the Atlantic to New York.

Titanic arrived at Cherbourg, anchoring in the roads between the moles at sunset; a perfect end to an eventful day.

Using the ship as a huge cross-Channel ferry, twenty-four passengers disembarked while 274 joiners were brought out to the ship; 142 had First-Class tickets; 30 had Second. The 102 Third-Class passengers represented many nationalities, many unable to speak or understand English.

First- and Second-Class passengers were ferried out to the liner in the new tender *Nomadic* (still in existence today, undergoing restoration in Belfast), which, with her consort *Traffic*, had been built by Harland and Wolff especially to service the new giants. It was in the latter vessel that Third Class and the new joiners' baggage was carried.

Thomas Andrews was pleased with the new tenders and wrote to his wife to say they 'looked well . . . we built them about a year ago'.

CHAIL 2007

69

Not only were emigrants making their way to the United States, but many wealthy and notable Americans and Canadians were returning home after perhaps spending the winter in warmer climes. Among this group was mining magnate Benjamin Guggenheim; the extremely wealthy 47-year-old John Jacob Astor IV (cousin to the anglicised William Waldorf Astor, later to become 1st Viscount Astor) and his 18-year-old pregnant wife, Madeline; their friend and travelling companion, Margaret 'Maggie' Brown, also embarked.

Maggie's estranged husband's wealth had arisen from his engineering efforts that had greatly assisted the exploitation of rich gold and copper seams in the United States, and now 'low-born' Maggie had been improving both her mind and social standing.

Travelling under the name of Morgan, the British Sir Cosmo and Lady Duff-Gordon (better known as Lucille, fashionable dress designer to the upper classes, including Queen Mary) also boarded.

The *Titanic* was now carrying wealthy industrialists, railwaymen and property tycoons, with many millionaires among them, as well as leading American socialites. The arts, too, were well represented. Author Jacques Futrelle (whose fictional character, The Thinking Machine, was a US version of Sherlock Holmes) and his wife; a star of the evolving cinema, Dorothy Gibson, boarded, as did American artist, correspondent and famed misogynist, Frank Millet, who would write acerbically of his fellow passengers: 'Queer lot of people on the ship . . . a number of obnoxious, ostentatious American women,

◄
Film star and Titanic *passenger Dorothy Gibson.* (Author's collection)

the scourge of any place they infest and worse on shipboard than anywhere.'

By 8 o'clock all was ready and secure, anchors were raised and the *Titanic*, brilliantly lit by hundreds of lights flooding from portholes and windows, headed out to sea towards Queenstown.

Lights-out was at 11.30 p.m., but the passengers needed no encouragement to retire after the excitements of the day and after an excellent dinner in all classes. Some thought that Third Class was as good as First on some of the older steamers.

During the course of the passage to Ireland, time was spent in exploring the ship. Third-Class passengers were not encouraged to visit areas other than their own due to US immigration laws and discouraged by waist-high 'Bostwick Gates' (mostly to avoid the spread of any contagious disease).

During the day, the ship's compasses were tested and some noted the changes in the ship's course. It is possible that the quartermasters were being given additional experience in handling the liner after *Olympic*'s collective dramas. A sharp ringing of bells informed the crew that the watertight doors were to be tested. The assurance given by these tests seemed to prove the press's assertions that the Olympic-class ships were 'unsinkable'.

After navigating St George's Channel, and picking up pilot John Whelan, *Titanic* arrived in the delightful roads of Queenstown, anchoring off Roche's Point at 11.30 a.m.

During the course of the morning, an excited crowd had congregated on the quayside near the White Star offices in readiness to be taken out to the liner. For

The Third-Class promenade area of the Poop Deck. (Cork Examiner)

The two tenders Ireland *and* America *at Queenstown.* (Cork Examiner)

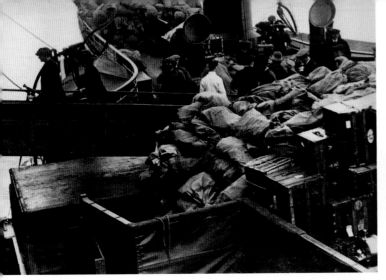

the greater part, the 123 people consisted of Irish, who, forsaking the poverty of their homeland, were emigrating to an anticipated better life, their lives distilled into a few precious suitcases and bundles.

There were Post Office officials ensuring that bags of mail were safely delivered to

Mail is off-loaded from the liner on to a waiting tender. (Fr Browne Collection/Davison & Associates Ltd, Dublin)

➤

The tender America *as seen from* Titanic's Boat Deck. (Cork Examiner)

> ➤
> *The anchors are weighed.*
> (Author's collection)

the ship (they would also bring several bags ashore containing final messages from those on board) and doctors who, as in Southampton and Cherbourg, would inspect the emigrants' health as they boarded before issuing a clearance certificate.

As the paddle steamer tenders *Ireland* and *America* brought baggage, mail, passengers and officials out to the liner many were startled to notice a blackened face peering down at them from the after (fourth) funnel. Some read this as a portent, but the face belonged to a trimmer who had climbed the dummy funnel's internal ladder to take the fresh air.

Just before 2 o'clock, with the captain looking over the ship's side from the starboard bridge wing to check that all was well, the two tenders departed.

The *Titanic*'s anchors were raised as she prepared to steam out of the anchorage.

Among the seven disembarking passengers was the Odell party and their guest, a young trainee from the Society of Jesus in Dublin, Father Francis Browne, who was possibly leaving the ship with some reluctance as, in response to his request to stay on board by invitation, had received short shrift from his Superior, the Provincial: 'Get off that ship.' The group took with them their precious cameras that had recorded their trips.

There was also an unauthorised passenger on a returning tender: deserting fireman John Coffey had hidden among the mailbags. He would return home to his mother but would soon be back at sea on the *Mauretania*.

As *Titanic* left Queenstown, emigrant Eugene Daly played *Erin's Lament* on his Irish pipes while looking over the ship's taffrail to a receding Ireland. The liner had just over 2,200 people on board; around 900 of whom were crew. Of the passengers, 324 were in First Class; around 280 in Second; and about 700 in Third. Cancellations had included Lord Pirrie (due to illness) and J. Pierpont Morgan, ensconced in his French château.

Those on board could now settle into their new surroundings, either enjoying the voyage as passengers or working as crew for the next six days.

As *Titanic* began her voyage across the Atlantic, those of the officers and crew without experience of the *Olympic* gradually became acclimatised to their huge new charge while carrying out their various duties. The passengers spent their time eating, sleeping, reading and exploring. In 1912 shipboard entertainments were few, but in First Class there were two bands: a trio who played in the à la carte restaurant

The port side of the verandah and Palm Court. The smoking room can be seen through the open doorway. (Ulster Folk & Transport Museum)

79

➤
Mabel Elvina Martin was employed as the second cashier in the elite à la carte restaurant. (By kind permission of the Estate of Mabel Elvina Martin)

➤➤
A bedroom in one of the period suites in First Class, this one decorated in the Empire style. (Ulster Folk & Transport Museum)

and a five-piece orchestra who played in the Palm Court or wherever required.

The à la carte restaurant was run by White Star and managed by Mr L. Gatti, formerly the manager of Oddenino's Imperial Restaurant in London's Regent Street.

First Class also had a library, a gymnasium (complete with instructor, Thomas McCawley), a swimming pool (one of the first afloat), a squash racquets court, a reading/writing room and even an ornate Turkish bath. Both the Turkish and swimming, or 'plunge', baths exercised a discreet segregation among their customers with ladies and gentlemen being allotted separate times. There were also passenger lifts: three in First Class and one in Second. Two barber-shops served the passengers, as did a surgery manned by two physicians.

Did you know?
Of the six or seven
dogs on board
Titanic when it sank,
three were saved.

FIRST SAILING OF THE LATEST ADDITION TO THE WHITE STAR FLEET

The Queen of the Ocean

TITANIC

LENGTH 882½ FT.   OVER 45,000 TONS   BEAM 92½ FT.
TRIPLE-SCREWS

This, the Latest, Largest and Finest Steamer Afloat, will sail from

WHITE STAR LINE, PIER 59 (North River), NEW YORK

Saturday, April 20th At 12 Noon

All passengers berthed in closed rooms
containing 2, 4, or 6 berths, a large number equipped with washstands, etc.

THIRD CLASS FOUR BERTH ROOM
Spacious Dining Saloons
Smoking Room
Ladies Reading Room
Covered Promenade

THIRD CLASS DINING SALOON

Reservations of Berths may be made direct with this Office or through any of our accredited Agents

THIRD CLASS RATES ARE:	
To PLYMOUTH, SOUTHAMPTON, LONDON, LIVERPOOL and GLASGOW.	$36.25
To GOTHENBURG, MALMÖ, CHRISTIANIA, COPENHAGEN, ESBJERG, Etc.	41.50
To STOCKHOLM, ÅBO, HANGÖ, HELSINGFORS	44.50
To HAMBURG, BREMEN, ANTWERP, AMSTERDAM, ROTTERDAM, HAVRE, CHERBOURG	45.00

TURIN, $48.   NAPLES, $52.50.   PIRAEUS, $55.   BEYROUTH, $61., Etc., Etc.

DO NOT DELAY: Secure your tickets through the local Agents or direct from

WHITE STAR LINE, 9 Broadway, New York

TICKETS FOR SALE HERE

The general decor of the ship was light and airy, being more 'Ritz hotel' in First Class than 'country house', which appealed greatly to the Americans. Light oak panelling, green patterned carpets and exquisite carving abounded. In comparison, the decor of the big Cunard liners appeared heavy, and the stuffy chintz of the German liners seemed an age away.

Second Class, also having a well-appointed library, could bask in surroundings that would not have shamed First Class on other liners.

Third Class, segregated with single men berthed forward, families and single women berthed aft, tended, as was expected, to look after themselves. The emigrants, especially from poorer regions of Europe – including Scandinavia – and the Near East, marvelled at the comparative luxury

Did you know?
Titanic had a gross
tonnage of 46,328
and could carry
around 2,400
passengers. The latest
cruise liner currently
being built, scheduled
for completion in
2009, is estimated
to weigh around
220,000gt and
will accommodate
5,400 people.

in which they found themselves. Wooden floors, white-painted walls and ceilings, electric lighting, running water, flushing toilets and regular meals with waiter service: these had been unobtainable luxuries in the 'old country'.

To pay for the huge social differences in accommodation, fares ranged from £6 10s in Third to over £900 for a First-Class suite for the seven-day passage. (£1 Stirling was valued at US $4.80 in 1912). In the stokehold, firemen or trimmers might earn £5 per month; a stewardess, £3 10s.

Titanic held within her hull a cross-section of the social make-up of the immediate post-Edwardian era, each part of which was very much aware of its position and of what it could expect from life. Those in Third Class, especially, were hoping that, within a few days, they would have the opportunity to expect much more than life had given them so far.

First Class performed as was expected of the higher echelons of the social strata with changes of dress to suit the hour: breakfast, morning, luncheon, afternoon, tea and, the grandest occasion of all, dinner, when the most elegant gowns and most brilliant jewels were worn by the women, accentuated by the gentlemen's attire of formal black-tailed dinner dress and starched white shirts.

The ship's staff carefully noted *Titanic*'s progress. The single-ended boilers in boiler room number 1 remained unlit for much of the voyage. It appeared that she was doing as well as, if not better than, the *Olympic* on her maiden voyage and it was hoped to fire the unlit boilers on the 15th. Coal was still plentiful on board and, although economy dictated its prudent use, it was hoped to push *Titanic* that day, probably meaning a Tuesday arrival in New York – in spite of her being advertised as a 'Wednesday boat'. But, even if she broke the *Olympic*'s maiden time, she could not approach the speed of Cunard's record-breakers.

The liner was approaching the south-flowing Labrador Current, which had its origins in currents from the eastern and western coasts of Greenland, bringing with them icebergs – some a decade or more old – calved from that great island's glaciers. These 'bergs then mixed with pack-ice floes formed from the broken sea ice of the previous winter and drifted southwards.

This mixed ice continued its relentless progress until it met the warm North Atlantic Drift, an extension of the Gulf Stream, coming from the tropics. At the meeting of

Part of the grand staircase. (Ulster Folk & Transport Museum)

The two Marconi operators – 'Jack' Phillips, First Wireless Operator, and Harold Bride, Second. (Fr Browne Collection/ Davison & Associates Ltd, Dublin)

cold and warm waters fog often developed and the melting of the ice accelerated. The seasonal shipping routes took into account the southern drift of ice, but still a quantity managed to survive its way into the busy shipping lanes. Ever vigilant ice reports were exchanged between ships that had wireless. Larger vessels often had two wireless operators, working a 24-hour watch; smaller vessels had just one operator and a correspondingly shorter watch.

The two operators on *Titanic* had been kept busy with private messages as, being employed by the Marconi Company, these were their *raison d'étre*. Messages for the ship were taken to the bridge as a courtesy.

By the 12th, the first few reports of ice were received and sent to the bridge but, later that evening, the apparatus (which had a range of at least 500 miles; up to 2,000

miles on a still night) had malfunctioned. Taking 6 hours to repair, it left the operators with a backlog of work.

Ice warnings continued to be received over the following two days. As *Titanic* approached the Labrador Current several such messages were received, being posted in the chart room for the information of the navigators. Meanwhile, on the 14th, the captain held Sunday Divine Service in the

First-Class dining room and, as all classes were invited to attend, the Third-Class passengers must have marvelled at the opulence of the surroundings in which they found themselves.

Just before 6 p.m. that day, *Titanic* approached the 47th Meridian where she would change course at 42° North from S62°W to S86°W, a point on the Great Circle route known as 'The Corner'.

It was apparent from the combined messages that there was a lot of ice ahead. The captain consequently ordered a course that would take her 20 miles further south of The Corner in order to avoid the reported obstacles.

Air temperatures began to fall: 43°F at 7 p.m; 39°F half-an-hour later.

Later that evening Captain Smith attended a dinner held in his honour, during

'As long as the weather is clear I always go full speed.'

Captain John Pritchard, retired captain of the Blue Ribband holder *Mauretania*.

which he asked Bruce Ismay to return an ice message from the *Baltic*. Posting this in the chart room just before 9 p.m., the captain discussed the prevailing conditions with Second Officer Lightoller and asked to be summoned should the conditions prove at all doubtful.

The moonless night was very cold but clear and there was not a breath of wind that could create a wash to give away the presence of any of the reported ice.

The extremely calm sea was, as Lightoller would recall, 'like glass'. The air temperature was, by now, just above freezing.

Second Officer Lightoller instructed the carpenter to check the fresh water tanks and the lookouts to keep a sharp watch for ice – even a 'black' 'berg (one that had recently capsized or broken off a parent and had not yet developed a coating of reflective crystals) should be relatively easy to spot, even at night. The crow's nest binoculars had been removed or locked away in Southampton as it was thought they only gave a tunnel vision instead of an all-round view.

Titanic was steaming at nearly 22.5 knots. Through custom and practice, and because of the night's clarity, it was not considered necessary to reduce the speed that had been increased during the day.

At 9.40 p.m. a message was received from the Atlantic Transport Line's *Mesaba*: 'Lat 42 N to 41.25 N, Longitude 40 W to 50.30 W, saw much heavy pack ice and great number large icebergs, also field ice.'

Due to the heavy volume of private traffic this message was 'spiked', awaiting later delivery to the bridge; a delivery that would not take place.

The watch changed at 10 p.m. as First Officer Murdoch relieved Lightoller. Junior Officers Boxhall and Moody had earlier succeeded their counterparts.

By 11.30 p.m. stewards had prepared tables for breakfast; the last passengers had retired and the ship was closed down for the night. In the boiler and engine rooms sweating firemen and trimmers went about their hot, grimy, never-ending toil of feeding the furnaces while engineers checked steam pressures, adjusted valves and tended to the smooth running of their machinery.

▲
The Crow's Nest key was one of several that survived the sinking. (Courtesy of Henry Aldridge & Son, Auctioneers, Devizes)

High up in the foremast crow's nest, above the line of sight of the navigators on the bridge, two lookouts – Fred Fleet and Reginald Lee – peered ahead into the night's freezing wind. A haze lingered on the horizon.

Then, at 11.40 p.m., Fleet saw a dark shape ahead of him; 'the size of two small tables'. As the shape approached and increased in size, he turned to the ship's bell, rang it sharply three times and reached for the telephone: 'What do you see?' answered Sixth Officer Moody on the bridge.

'Iceberg, right ahead!' shouted Fleet into the instrument.

'Thank you!' came an almost calm reply.

Moody hurriedly repeated the call to Murdoch who shouted, 'Hard a-starboard!' He ordered the engine room telegraphs to indicate 'Full Astern' and pressed the switch that remotely closed the watertight doors. His intention was to then hard-a-port after reversing the engines and swerve around the 'berg thus swinging the ship's stern clear.

Thirty seconds of tense concentration ensued, waiting for the orders to take effect. The propellers thrashed, taking the way off the ship with a resultant lack of water flow over the rudder, somewhat reducing manoeuvrability.

The iceberg rapidly approached, gaining in height when, at the last moment, the ship's bow arced to port. The 'berg glided by. Shards of ice tumbled onto the fore Well Deck.

When a ship's bow turns into a turning circle its stern swings out, so it is possible that, not only did the ship graze her underwater bow along the 'berg in a series of contacts – perhaps five or six – that opened plate seams and popped rivets, but a projection of the 'berg could have hit her bottom further aft before Murdoch's plan had time to take effect.

▲ Titanic *turns to head down Southampton Water.* (Author's collection)

At the sound of activity Captain Smith hurriedly appeared on the bridge as *Titanic* drifted to a stop. Murdoch reported the events and orders of the preceding minute before the captain sent the Fourth Officer on a tour of inspection. Boxhall returned to report that nothing seemed to be amiss. The ship was ordered ahead at half-speed, but came to a halt 5 minutes later. Thomas Andrews was summoned.

Boxhall was sent on another inspection but met the ship's carpenter, John Hutchinson, rushing to the bridge: 'She's making water fast!'

Andrews and the captain conducted their own tour. The five postal clerks had started moving bags of registered mail out of the rapidly flooding lower part of the mail room but, within minutes, water had risen to the second level.

Just before midnight Andrews quickly calculated five damaged compartments: forepeak, numbers 1 and 2 holds, the mail room and boiler room number 6, all filling rapidly. Pumps were controlling the water in the sixth compartment, boiler room number 5.

With the ship already listing 5 degrees to starboard and 2 degrees down by the head, Andrews surmised that the water in the

flooding compartments would pull the bow down further, causing water to overflow into the next compartment aft and so on; a simple matter of progression.

He informed the captain that *Titanic* had only an hour, perhaps an hour-and-a-half at the most, to live. Her lifeboat capacity was for 1,186 people; there were 2,208 on board.

From that point on, 2 hours of desperate struggle would ensue (times are approximate):

12.02 a.m. Captain gives orders to prepare the lifeboats for lowering and to muster the passengers and crew.

12.10 a.m. Captain personally takes the first wireless message requesting assistance to the Marconi room and 4 minutes later returns to tell the operators to transmit: 'CQD 41°46'N, 50°24'W.' The message is transmitted several times before the position is corrected to 41°46'N, 50°14'W and is followed by: 'Require immediate assistance. We have collision with iceberg. Sinking.'

At that moment *Titanic*'s operators were unable to hear any responses as the safety valves on the funnels were venting steam. But her messages were picked up by several ships. Some requested further details and asked if *Titanic* was steaming towards them, perhaps misunderstanding an earlier message when the captain reported that he had moved a few miles ahead after the collision.

12.45 a.m. MGY (*Titanic*'s call sign) changes from CQD to the relatively new SOS in a message to *Olympic*: 'I require immediate assistance.'

The first lifeboat, No. 7, is lowered as the first of eight rockets sear the night sky in a

desperate attempt to attract a ship whose lights can be seen 6 miles away. A Morse lamp is used to no avail.

Above and below decks, human dramas were constantly being played out. 'Women and children first!' was an order strenuously observed by Second Officer Lightoller, although families were sometimes allowed into other boats. Some husbands declined a place, as did Thomas Brown who, after seeing his wife and daughter into a boat, stepped back, calling: 'I'll see you in New York!'

Mrs Straus and other wives refused to leave their husbands. Elsewhere whole families, including the seven-strong Goodwin family stayed united. Some boats got away completely full, others painfully less so.

Most of the responding ships were too far away to be of assistance but relayed messages to others. One ship, the Cunard liner RMS *Carpathia*, was on her way from New York to the Mediterranean. Turning about at the first summons, she was 58 miles and 4 hours away – 2 hours too far.

01.40 a.m. After detonation intervals of 8–10 minutes the last rocket is fired.

01.45 a.m. *Carpathia* picks up *Titanic*'s last audible signal: 'Engine room full up to bunkers.'

◄◄
Boats are lowered from Titanic. *(Author's collection)*

◄
A dramatic illustration by Fortunino Matania showing the passengers' differing reactions as they realise there are so few boats. (The Mariners' Museum, Newport News, Virginia, USA)

01.50 a.m. Forepeak dips under the sea, hastening the final act.

01.55 a.m. Foredeck submerges and the propellers rise above the surface.

02.05 a.m. Englehardt collapsible Boat D becomes the last boat to be launched from the davits. Due to stresses in the superstructure the forward expansion joint opens enough for the stays to the forward funnel to taughten and break. The funnel falls forward and to starboard, crushing in its path not only the bridge wing cabin but several people struggling in the water.

02.10 a.m. The wireless operators are released by Captain Smith and abandon

'Ah! But do you remember the silence that followed it?'

Eva Hart quoting her mother.

An illustration of Titanic's final moments from The Graphic *by Charles Dixon. (Author's collection)*

John Jacob Astor (left) here seen at the 1911 Derby, would remain on board after seeing his wife into a lifeboat. (The Sphere, 10 June 1911)

their room only a few minutes after a last desperate attempt at transmitting.

Of various groups of people on the ship, the mail room clerks heroically tried their best to rescue the mail; musicians, under leader Wallace Hartley, also behaved in an exemplary fashion. Earlier on during the crisis they had played lively music to help keep spirits up, perhaps too successfully as many passengers refused to believe that there was anything amiss with the ship. Finally, as the ship's stern rose higher, they played a final piece which Hartley had said he would like played when his end came; the hymn, *Nearer My God to Thee*.

As music drifted serenely across a still-calm, pitch-black sea dotted with sixteen lifeboats and collapsibles (one still remained on the ship and would be launched upside down in the final moments that were now not far off) an incredible sight presented itself to those in the boats. Rows of bright lights still burned on the liner; those at the forward end were submerged, those remaining in view were angled acutely to the mill-pond ocean.

At around 02.18 a.m. the stern rose into a sky brilliantly lit by stars. As the bow sank deeper the lights went out, flashing briefly before being extinguished for ever. At this point, when the stern was perhaps at 40 degrees to the surface of the sea, the hull began to rupture. The bow continued to sink as the stern began to split from the main hull, just abaft the third funnel. The fracture might have been caused by a point of damage on the ship's bottom that, combined with stresses on the after expansion joint, created the start of a catastrophic failure.

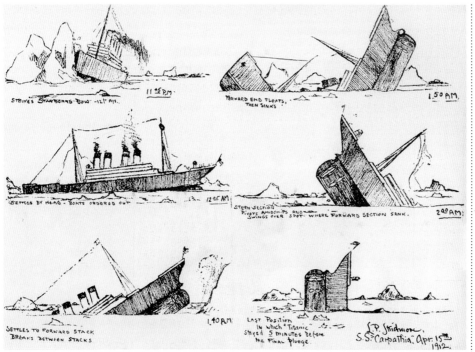

STRIKES STARBOARD BOW - 11:45 P.M.

11:45 P.M.

FORWARD END FLOATS, THEN SINKS

1:50 A.M.

SETTLES BY HEAD - BOATS ORDERED OUT

12:05 A.M.

STERN SECTION PIVOTS AMIDSHIPS AND SWINGS OVER SPOT WHERE FORWARD SECTION SANK.

2:00 A.M.

SETTLES TO FORWARD STACK BREAKS BETWEEN STACKS

1:40 A.M.

LAST POSITION IN WHICH "TITANIC" STAYED 5 MINUTES BEFORE THE FINAL PLUNGE.

L.P. Skidmore, S.S. "Carpathia" Apr. 15th 1912.

◄

A sketch of Titanic's *sinking by L.P. Skidmore, based on descriptions given by survivor John B. Thayer Jnr.* (Illustrated London News, 11 May 1912)

As the bow sank, pulling the still-buoyant stern after it, a buckling effect occurred as the stern pushed the submerged fore end further down, causing compression along the upper decks. The bow sank further, still joined to its neighbour by an umbilical of keel, until it pulled the still-fairly-buoyant stern into an almost vertical position. The submerged weight severed the keel, leaving the stern to float for what seemed to be minutes, held upright by the weight of the engines.

Gradually the stern lost its remaining buoyancy, settling slightly back before making its final descent. Due to its fineness, the bow section descended at an angle, but the heavier stern sank like a stone, imploding as it plunged to the depths.

Two miles down the bow impacted with the seabed at an angle before sliding

Did you know?
Proportionally, more First-Class male passengers were saved than Third-Class children.

THE TITANIC SUNK!

COLLISION WITH AN ICEBERG.

HUGE DEATH ROLL.

SOUTHAMPTON IN MOURNING.

ROYAL SYMPATHY WITH THE BEREAVED.

RELIEF FUNDS OPENED.

THE ILLUSTRATED LONDON NEWS, April 20, 1912.—591

CRAVING NEWS OF "TITANIC" PASSENGERS: AT WHITE STAR OFFICES.

horizontally along the silt, coming to rest upright. The adjoining structure aft was still at an angle, buckling as the bow impacted and split the hull just below the bridge. Half a mile away the stern landed heavily, the Poop Deck peeled back like a can's lid. In between the two major wreckage sites, coal and debris littered the seabed.

On the surface, 2 miles above, and after the cries of those freezing in the water had subsided, the survivors awaited rescue. *Carpathia* was sighted just after 3.30 a.m. following her noble dash through the night. It took 4 hours to pick up the survivors, the count of whom totalled 705.

True to form, the wages of the crew were stopped from the time of the sinking.

In the aftermath, there followed a homecoming and a realisation that life had changed, not only for the rescued but for all who would go to sea in the future.

American and British inquiries were held and, from both, legislation came into being to ensure that the shortcomings that befell *Titanic* would not befall ships that followed. Among many changes, an International Ice Patrol was formed to monitor icebergs as they approached the shipping lanes; 'Lifeboats for all' became the watchword.

A telegram informs a family that their loved one did not survive. (Southampton City Museums)

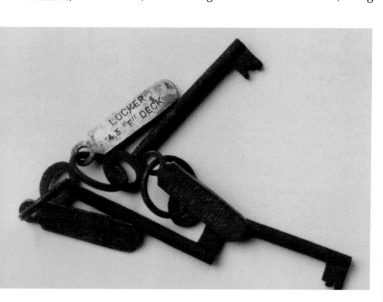

▼
A set of locker keys recovered from the body of 31-year-old Saloon Steward Robert Bristow. (Southampton City Museums)

*T*itanic remained undiscovered for nearly seventy-five years. An occasional cinema film was made of the disaster but it was not until 1957, when Walter Lord wrote *A Night to Remember* which, along

with a film of the same name, once again focused the world's attention on the event. Following this renewed interest came an ambition to find the wreck and this was realised in September 1985, when the American part of a joint French-American expedition discovered *Titanic*.

From this a veritable 'Titanic industry' has grown with aspects of the disaster being studied by specialist societies, books, films, TV documentaries and computer websites all over the world.

Mystery still surrounds her story: which was the ship that lay within 6 miles of her foundering? Was it the *Californian* or was she 20 miles away as has been claimed?

As the 100th anniversary approaches, the fascination with the disaster shows no sign of abating.

◄◄
Appreciative medals were presented to the crew of Carpathia, *including Fourth Officer Geoffrey Barnish.* (By kind permission of the Estate of Geoffrey Barnish)

◄
A young Geoffrey Barnish who became Fourth Officer of Carpathia. (By kind permission of the Estate of Geoffrey Barnish)

Length overall:	882ft 9in
Length between perpendiculars:	850ft
Breadth extreme:	92ft 6in
Draught:	34ft 6in
Gross Tonnage:	46,328
Displacement:	Around 52,250 tons
Height from keel to navigating bridge:	104ft
Height from keel to top of funnels:	175ft
Decks:	9 in total including Orlop Decks
Hull construction:	1½-inch thick plate steel at keel
Rivets:	3 million (approx. 65% wrought iron, manually applied, and 35% mild steel, machine applied)
Power plant:	29 coal-fired boilers using 825 tons of coal per day. Three of the funnels were used for exhaust; the fourth was 'dummy' venting for *Titanic*'s kitchens and galleys. The funnels were 22ft wide and 62ft high
Engines:	2 reciprocating 4-cylinder steam engines produced 30,000hp at 75rpm for the 2 wing

➤➤

A section through the Olympic-class liners.
(Illustrated London News, 20 April 1912)

propellers. One low-pressure Parsons Turbine produced 16,000hp to drive the centre propeller at 165rpm. The turbine was powered by exhausted steam from the 2 reciprocating engines

Propellers:	2 wing propellers of 23ft 6in diameter and 1 centre propeller of 16ft 6in diameter
Official Number:	131428
Port of registry:	Liverpool
Anchors:	1 centre anchor weighing 15¾ tons and 2 side (bower) anchors at nearly 8 tons
Top speed:	24 knots at 75rpm
Passengers:	Maximum: 739 First Class, 674 Second Class and 1,026 Third Class. On her maiden voyage there were 329 First Class, 285 Second Class and 710 Third Class
Crew:	892; 7 officers plus the captain
Lifeboat capacities:	2 x 40 persons 'emergency' lifeboats; 14 x 65 persons wooden lifeboats; 4 x 49 persons Engelhardt collapsible boats

➤➤
Titanic's 15¾ ton centre anchor. (Author's collection)

109

110

Lifesaving appliances: 3,560 life belts and 48 life rings

Cost to build: £2 million

Provisions, Dining Room and Galley Equipment:

57,600 kitchen items (pots, pans, etc.)

29,000 items of glassware

44,000 pieces of cutlery

75,000 lb fresh meat

11,000 lb fresh fish

4,000 lb salted and dried fish

7,500 lb bacon and ham

25,000 lb poultry

40,000 fresh eggs

2,500 lb sausages

40 tons potatoes

3,500 lb onions

800 bundles of fresh asparagus

3,500 lb tomatoes

2,500 lb peas

7,000 heads of lettuce

1,000 loaves of bread

2,200 lb ground coffee

800 lb tea

10,000 lb rice and dried beans

10,000 lb sugar

250 barrels of flour

10,000 lb cereal

36,000 apples

36,000 oranges

16,000 lemons

1,000 lb grapes

13,000 grapefruit

1,120 lb jam and marmalade

1,500 gallons of fresh milk

1,200 quarts of ice cream

600 gallons of condensed milk

6,000 lb butter

15,000 bottles of beers and lagers

1,000 bottles of wine

850 bottles of spirits

14,000 gallons of fresh water daily

◀◀
Sliding the starboard shaft into its bossing prior to fitting the propeller. (Ulster Folk & Transport Museum)

111

Anderson, Roy, *White Star*, Prescot, T. Stephenson & Sons Ltd, 1964

Bonsor, N.R.P., *North Atlantic Seaway* Vols 1 and 2, Newton Abbot, David and Charles, 1975

Chernow, Ron, *The House of Morgan: An American Banking Dynasty and the Rise of Modern Finance*, Touchstone, 1990

Eaton, John P. and Haas, Charles A., *Titanic – Triumph and Tragedy: A Chronicle in Words and Pictures*, Wellingborough, Patrick Stephens Ltd, 1986

—— *Titanic: A Journey Through Time*, Wellingborough, Patrick Stephens Ltd, 1999

Green, Rod, *Building the Titanic*, London, Carlton Books, 1996

Grice, Bob Bruce and Hutchings, David F., *Southampton Shipping – with Portsmouth, Poole and Weymouth*, London, Carmania Press, 2006

Haisman, David, *I'll See You in New York – Titanic: the Courage of a Survivor*, Brisbane, Boolarong Press, 1999

Hutchings, David F., *Titanic: 75 Years of Legend* (later *A Modern Legend*), Settle, Kingfisher Railway Productions, 1987 (Ninth impression 2004)

MacQuitty, William, *A Life to Remember*, London, Quartet Books, 1991

McCaughan, Michael, *The Birth of Titanic*, Belfast, The Blackstaff Press, 1998

McCluskie, Tom, *Anatomy of the Titanic*, London, PRC Publishing Ltd, 1998

Mills, Simon, *RMS Olympic: The Old Reliable*, Blandford Forum, Waterfront Publications, 1993

Moss, Michael and Hume, John R., *Shipbuilders to the World: 125 Years of Harland and Wolff, Belfast 1861–1986*, Belfast and Wolfeboro, NH, The Blackstaff Press, 1986

Oldham, Wilton J., *The Ismay Line*, Liverpool, The Journal of Commerce, 1961

Robertson, Morgan, *Futility or The Wreck of the Titan*, Riverside, CT, 7 C's Press Inc., 1974

Shipbuilder, *Ocean Liners of the Past: 'Olympic' & 'Titanic'*, London, Patrick Stephens Ltd, 1970

Ticehurst, Brian, *The Crew of the RMS Titanic: Who Were They?* Southampton City Council, 2006

Wilkinson, Norman, *A Brush With Life*, London, Seeley Service & Co. Ltd, 1969

Woodman, Richard, *The Real Cruel Sea*, London, John Murray, 2005

▼
Titanic on her maiden voyage, sailing past Cowes on the Isle of Wight on her way to Cherbourg, a curl of steam exuding from her forward funnel to warn an approaching tug. (Author's collection)

S. S. "TITANIC," 46,000 TONS.
hich Struck an Iceberg, on her maiden voyage, Sunday 14th April, 1912, and foundered with the loss of 1,500 li

Other Sources:

Hutchings, David F., *Titanic – The Worldly Hope* (lecture)

Stoker, Bram, *The World's Greatest Shipbuilding Yard*, extract from the US periodical, *The World's Work*, New York, Scribner & Son, 1907

www.encyclopedia-titanic.org
www.titanicinternationalsociety.org
www.titanic-nautical.com/titanic-facts
(Facts and Figures are based on information from this website to which acknowledgement is gratefully made.)